AMAZING WONDERS

EGYPTIAN PYRAMIDS

BY HEIDI NEWBAUER

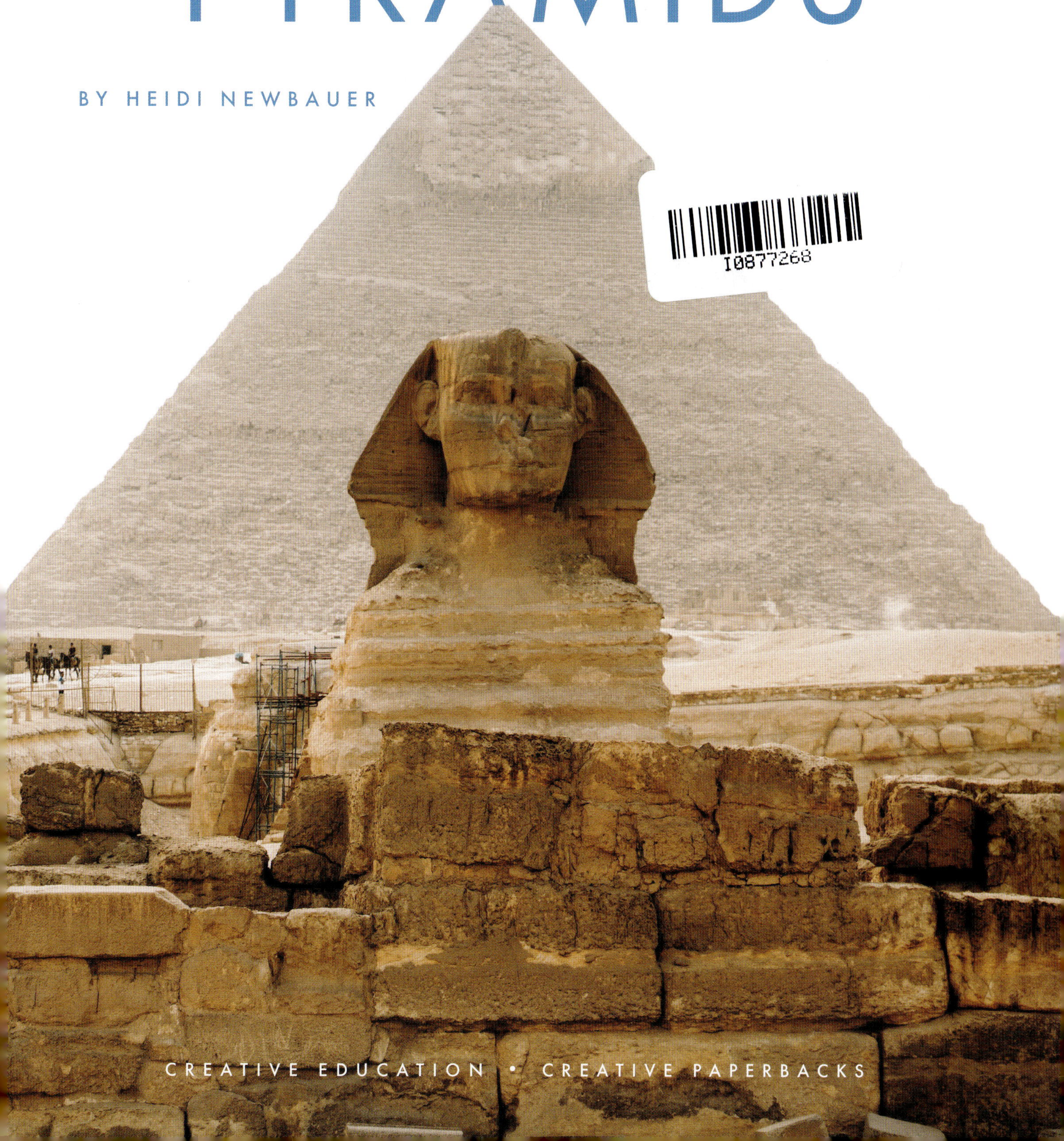

CREATIVE EDUCATION • CREATIVE PAPERBACKS

Published by Creative Education and Creative Paperbacks
P.O. Box 227, Mankato, Minnesota 56002
Creative Education and Creative Paperbacks
are imprints of The Creative Company
www.thecreativecompany.us

Design by The Design Lab
Art direction by Graham Morgan
Edited by Jill Kalz

Images by Getty (KHALED DESOUKI/AFP, Universal History Archive), Pexels (Mostafa El Shershaby, Oziel Gómez), Unsplash (Alex Azabache, Andreea Munteanu, Andrés Dallimonti, AXP Photography, Hossam M. Omar, Robert Thiemann, Steffen Gundermann, Sumit Mangela)

Library of Congress Cataloging-in-Publication Data
Names: Newbauer, Heidi, author.
Title: Egyptian pyramids / Heidi Newbauer.
Other titles: Amazing wonders (Creative Education, Inc. (Mankato, Minn.))
Description: Mankato, MN : Creative Education and Creative Paperbacks, 2025. | Series: Amazing wonders | Includes bibliographical references and index. | Audience: Ages 6–9 | Audience: Grades 2–3 | Summary: "An elementary-level introduction to the ancient Egyptian pyramids, covering how, when, and why the famous wonders were built. Includes captions, on-page definitions, additional resources, and an index"—Provided by publisher.
Identifiers: LCCN 2023042428 (print) | LCCN 2023042429 (ebook) | ISBN 9781640268586 (library binding) | ISBN 9781682774083 (paperback) | ISBN 9798889890201 (ebook)
Subjects: LCSH: Pyramids—Egypt—Juvenile literature.
Classification: LCC DT63 .N49 2025 (print) | LCC DT63 (ebook) | DDC 932/.012—dc23/eng/20231107
LC record available at https://lccn.loc.gov/2023042428
LC ebook record available at https://lccn.loc.gov/2023042429

Printed in China

Table of Contents

The largest of the three Pyramids of Giza was built for King Khufu (c. 2575–c. 2465 BC).

The pyramids of Egypt are large ancient structures made of bricks and stone. They were built to hold the bodies of pharaohs. There are more than 100 Egyptian pyramids. The biggest three are called the Pyramids of Giza.

pharaohs ancient kings of Egypt

Egypt is a country in northern Africa. It is mostly desert. The Nile River is its main water source. Many of the best-known pyramids lie near the Nile and the city of Cairo.

The Nile is the longest river in the world, at 4,160 miles (6,695 kilometers).

The first Egyptian pyramid was built around 2630 BC. It was the final resting place of King Djoser. Most of the Egyptian pyramids were built between 2613 and 2494 BC.

The Great Pyramid of Giza was built more than 4,500 years ago.

Building a pyramid was very difficult work. People made bricks by hand. They gathered and cut heavy rock called limestone. Some of the stones were brought from far away by ancient waterways.

Builders left behind no plans to show how they made such perfect shapes.

The Great Pyramid of Giza was built with an estimated 2.3 million stone blocks.

The pyramid stones were dragged up a ramp by **pulleys**. Each new layer of the pyramid got smaller and smaller. The top stone came to a point. It was called a capstone.

pulleys simple machines used to move or lift heavy objects

Near the Great Pyramid of Giza is a half-man, half-lion statue called the Great Sphinx.

Thousands of people built the pyramids. **Enslaved** people did much of the heavy work. The Great Pyramid of Giza took about 20 years to build. At that pace, workers would have delivered, cut, and set 34 large stones every day.

enslaved forced to work without pay or freedom

Bodies were wrapped in cloth bandages after they were preserved.

The bodies inside the pyramids were **mummified**. People placed riches such as gold and jewels with the bodies. The objects were meant to protect the dead person's spirit. They were also meant to protect that person's family.

mummified preserved for burial in Egyptian times

Archeologists dig and chip away earth to uncover buried objects.

The mask of an Egyptian mummy

The pyramids of Egypt hold many mysteries. **Archeologists** use computers and other tools to learn more about them. They study the building process. They study how things were stored and kept safe inside the structures.

archeologists people who study history through the things people left behind

The pyramids of Egypt have stood for thousands of years. They are beautiful wonders to look at. But they also teach us an important lesson: Even if a difficult task takes time, it is possible to do it!

More than 14 million people visit the pyramids each year.

Wonder Spotlight: Sarcophagus

A sarcophagus is a type of coffin that sits above ground. The mummified body of a pharaoh rests inside. Every pyramid holds at least one sarcophagus, each in its own room. Although many of these coffins were made of gold, some were made of stone and wood. Every sarcophagus is different. No two are the same.

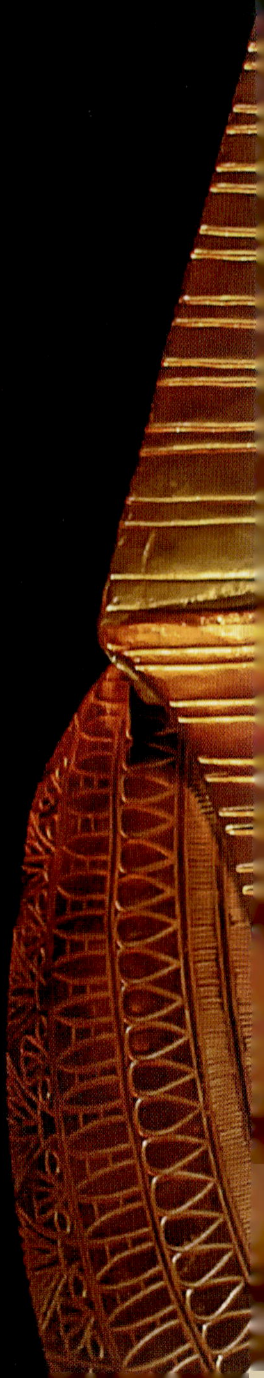

Read More

Alexander, Heather. *A Child's Introduction to Egyptology: The Mummies, Pyramids, Pharaohs, Gods, and Goddesses of Ancient Egypt*. New York: Black Dog & Leventhal Publishers, 2021.

Hart, George. *Ancient Egypt*. New York: DK Publishing, 2021.

Honovich, Nancy. *1,000 Facts about Ancient Egypt*. Washington, D.C.: National Geographic, 2019.

Websites

Britannica Kids: Ancient Egypt
https://kids.britannica.com/kids/article/Ancient-Egypt/353087
Learn about life in Ancient Egypt.

National Geographic Kids: Ancient Egypt
https://kids.nationalgeographic.com/history/article/ancient-egypt
Learn more about the dynasties of Ancient Egypt.

Index